MEERKAT
MOVES OUT
of the DESERT

by Nikki Potts • illustrated by Maarten Lenoir

PICTURE WINDOW BOOKS
a capstone imprint

Meerkats, meerkats everywhere!

Meerkats live together in burrows underground.

Baby meerkats. Mama meerkats. Daddy meerkats. Meerkat cousins.

Too many meerkats!

Meerkat wants some time alone. She needs her own place.

But where
should she go?

THIS WAY
OUT

The mountains!
It is much quieter here.

A little too quiet . . .

YIKES!
Meerkat has
caused an avalanche!

RUN!

Meerkat scurries as fast as she can.

WHOOSH!

She dives into an empty cave.

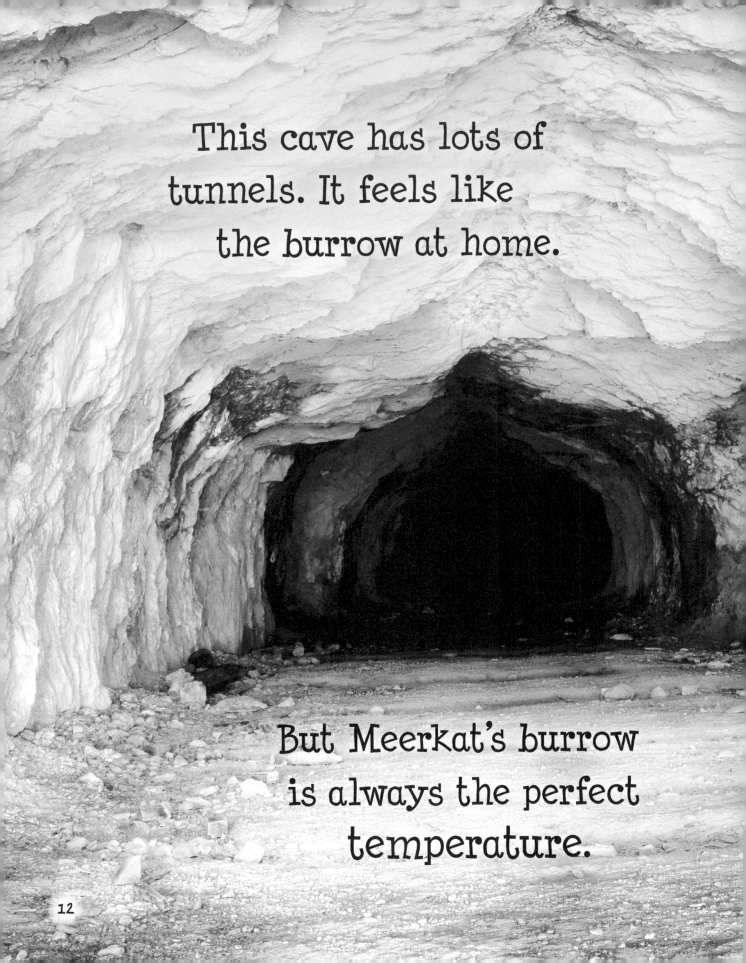

This cave has lots of tunnels. It feels like the burrow at home.

But Meerkat's burrow is always the perfect temperature.

Caves are much too cold.

BRRRR!

Meerkat thought
she was alone.
Then she
looked up.

Maybe she
can find a
new friend!

Meerkat is not ready
to make that many
new friends!

The mountains were
not the right home
for Meerkat.

A cave was not the
right home either.

Will Meerkat ever
find the perfect
place to live?

Look at all these tunnels! This park could be the perfect place to live.

The monkey bars are too high!

OUCH!
The plastic slide is too hot!

This playground is
not the right habitat
for Meerkat.

Maybe a garden will be a nice place to live.

Now this is relaxing!

22

It is quiet here.
The plants are pretty.

There is plenty to eat.

And the dirt
is cool and soft.

The dirt is TOO soft!

Meerkat cannot
dig a burrow.

Without a burrow,
how will Meerkat
stay safe?

Meerkat misses the dry burrows.
She misses the hard dirt
that is perfect for tunneling.

She misses being warm.
She misses the noise.
Most of all, she misses
her family.

It is time
for Meerkat to
go home.

Everyone was waiting for Meerkat. That was a lot of waiting!

Welcome Home!

Welcome home, Meerkat!

ALL ABOUT MEERKATS

Meerkats only go outside during the day.

Meerkats have a very good sense of smell.

Adult meerkats take turns staying in the burrow to watch new pups.

Meerkat burrows have multiple entrances and exits.

A sentry is a meerkat who stands on a high point and watches for danger.

Meerkats hiss and show their teeth and claws when threatened.

ANIMAL PASSPORT

Name: Meerkat

Type: mammal

Habitat: desert

Diet: beetles, caterpillars, spiders, scorpions

Height: 11.4 inches (29 centimeters)

Weight: less than 2 pounds (1 kilogram)

Lifespan: 12 to 14 years

Favorite activity: cuddling

BOOKS IN THIS SERIES

Habitat Hunter is published by Picture Window Books, an imprint of Capstone.
1710 Roe Crest Drive
North Mankato, Minnesota 56003
www.capstonepub.com

Library of Congress Cataloging-in-Publication Data is available on the Library of Congress website.
ISBN: 978-1-9771-1419-8 (library binding)
ISBN: 978-1-9771-2017-5 (paperback)
ISBN: 978-1-9771-1425-9 (eBook PDF)

Summary: Meerkat is bored with its habitat! Follow Meerkat as it tries out different places to live. Which habitat will make the best home for Meerkat?

Image Credits
Shutterstock: Albert Russ, 12-13, Alessio Bonfanti, 16-17, Alexander Raths, 26-27, Artography, 18-19, Fabio Lamanna, cover, Lysogor Roman, 8-9, My Good Images, 10, natali_polskaya, 26-27, Oleksii Grygorenko, 6-7, PandG, 24-25, Pasko Maksim, 22-23, r.kathesi, 14, RAJU SONI, 28-29, 31, reisegraf.ch, 15, senee sriyota, 20-21, shymar27, 4, skapuka, 14, Stacey Newman, 20 (inset), sumroeng chinnapan, cover, superbank stock, 14, tratong, 2-3, Vector8DIY, backcover, Yuriy Kulik, 11

Artistic elements: pingebat, Valeriya_Dor

Editorial Credits
Editor: Mari Bolte; Designer: Kayla Rossow; Media Researcher: Kelly Garvin; Production Specialist: Tori Abraham

All internet sites appearing in back matter were available and accurate when this book was sent to press.